IMAGES
of America

TRAVELING THE
MERRITT
PARKWAY

D1529020

Congressman Schuler Merritt became the focal point around which community leaders joined forces to pressure the Connecticut Legislature to finance a new highway parallel to U.S. Route 1. Schuler Merritt graduated from Yale University in 1873, from Columbia University in 1876, and received an L.L.D. from Yale in 1935. He served the State of Connecticut in the Congress a total of nine terms (1917-1931, 1933-1937).

IMAGES
of America

TRAVELING THE
MERRITT
PARKWAY

Larry Larned

ARCADIA

First printed in 1998.
Reprinted in 2002.

Published by Arcadia Publishing,
an imprint of Tempus Publishing, Inc.
2A Cumberland Street
Charleston, SC 29401

Printed in Great Britain.
Library of Congress Catalog Card Number: 98-86559

For all general information contact Arcadia Publishing at:
Telephone 843-853-2070
Fax 843-853-0044
E-Mail sales@arcadiapublishing.com

For customer service and orders:
Toll-Free 1-888-313-2665

Visit us on the internet at http://www.arcadiapublishing.com

This view taken during 1931 shows U.S. Route 1 at the Connecticut/New York state line. A billboard on the right proclaims, "This is Greenwich The Gateway of New England." The four lanes of U.S. Route 1 are visible with a traffic survey being conducted at key station no. 6. Traffic surveys during this period revealed an average daily traffic volume of 4,492 vehicles, with a maximum of 8,000 vehicles on Sundays during the month of August. These statistics were used to support the need for constructing a parallel route to U.S. Route 1; this route in time became the Merritt Highway, followed by the Merritt Parkway.

CONTENTS

ACKNOWLEDGMENTS

Special thanks to Mary Clark, Gabrielle Esperdy, Joanne McAllister-Hewlings, Barbara Kier, Andree Larned, Robert Moore, B. Devon Perkins, David Ramson, John Roger, Jacqueline Salame, Corinne Smith, Todd Thibodeau, Christopher Wygren, the Stamford Historical Society, archives of the former Connecticut Highway Department (CHD), the Army National Guard, and the records of the Connecticut Department of Transportation.

INTRODUCTION

Following World War II Americans took to the road embarking on family vacations to destinations requiring journeys by car over roads they would long remember. The Merritt Parkway is one of these roads. Built as a bypass to U.S. Route 1 through southern Connecticut, the Merritt was crowned Queen of the Parkways and remains a road like no other anywhere in the United States. It continues to serve as a gateway to New England and, since its full opening on Labor Day 1940, has carried millions of people to distant points in New England including Cape Cod and Maine. Vacationers and businesspeople alike have driven the Merritt Parkway as an experience fulfilling the best intentions of its designers, who incorporated a theatrical theme over its 37-mile length.

Construction of the Merritt Parkway was begun during 1934 in Greenwich. This followed the beginning of construction for the Merritt Highway in Stratford during 1932. The transition from highway to parkway marked a turning point during an era of road construction in Connecticut. Building the Merritt was a final chapter in a scheme to alleviate congestion on nearby U.S. Route 1, particularly for travelers wishing to pass through Connecticut to other New England points. Other chapters in this development included the construction of Route 80, a road which served as the model for the Merritt Highway, but lacked the aesthetic qualities of the Merritt Parkway.

The section of Merritt Highway being constructed in Stratford during 1932 created an undercurrent of animosity along the projected route to Greenwich caused by a lack of aesthetic qualities. Citizen groups were formed to fight the approved design. But Fairfield County lacked a plan of its own to offer the State. Believing the State would continue its standard Route 80-type design, concerned residents of Fairfield County formed the Fairfield County Planning Association, Inc., known locally as the FCPA. The association's goal was to adopt a plan to include a parkway design from Greenwich to Stratford and to convince the Merritt Parkway Commission, chaired by Congressman Schuler Merritt of Stamford, that this highway project should reflect the cultural and social values of Fairfield County. Legislation was passed changing the routing of the road directly east of the Housatonic River. A new bridge was authorized to carry traffic over the river and to the east and north. The Merritt Highway became the Merritt Parkway, to be enjoyed by countless travelers fascinated by the lure of a road conveying a marriage of engineering and aesthetics.

Dedication

To the people who made the Parkway what it is.

One

GREENWICH

Its narrow character made widening U.S. Route 1 through Greenwich difficult. Shown above is a two-lane section of U.S. Route 1 during 1929 at the Byram River. The same traffic conditions affecting Connecticut were affecting New York too. The Hutchinson River Parkway—completed during 1936 to 1939 and ending at Purchase Street in Port Chester—was considered a partial solution to severe traffic problems on U.S. Route 1 from New Rochelle to Port Chester. Connecticut's solution was similar—an inland highway devoted to moving passenger traffic, the Merritt Parkway.

Traffic analysis during 1931 was accomplished by individuals observing separate lanes of travel. Some cars were stopped and the drivers asked questions about the nature of their trip. This scene shows a team collecting traffic statistics at the Connecticut/New York state line on U.S. Route 1. Their traffic data was used for determining the exit and entrance locations for the Parkway. Following the full opening of the Parkway during 1940, similar counts were conducted for determining the percentage of interstate traffic still using U.S. Route 1.

The motor vehicle department traffic counting team monitors travel at a traffic survey point on U.S. Route 1 in Greenwich during 1931. Surveys of this nature, used to support the need for highway improvements, were developed in compliance with the 1921 Federal Highway Act. The Boston Post Road became U.S. Route 1 during 1926 when a uniform system of guide signs was adopted for use on interstate routes in all states. Improving these routes, including U.S. Route 1 through Connecticut, became a national priority.

The King Street Underpass straddling the Connecticut/New York state line frames a panoramic view of Greenwich on the Merritt Parkway during 1949. The underpass was constructed by the State of New York and partially financed by the State of Connecticut. This structure is of rigid-frame construction and reflects neither the typical Hutchinson River Underpass nor the typical Merritt Parkway Underpass. Rather, the King Street Underpass is modeled on the Bronx-Whitestone Bridges under construction during 1936 to 1939.

COMMERCIAL VEHICLES
TAXICABS TRAILERS
PEDESTRIANS PROHIBITED
ON MERRITT PARKWAY
MERRITT PARKWAY COMMISSION

NO PICNICKING
ALLOWED ON PARKWAY

YOU ARE ENTERING

CONNECTICUT

ON THE

MERRITT PARKWAY

The first completed stretch of the Parkway extended from this point for a length of 18.5 miles to U.S. Route 7 in Norwalk. Signage on the Parkway was unique and provided a rustic charm. Exit numbers were added during June 1947, with King Street being designated as Exit 27. The numbering system was developed in cooperation with Westchester County parkway officials,

who established the first 26 exits on the Hutchinson River Parkway in New York. During 1955 the entrance ramps were reconstructed to eliminate the sharp turns appearing in this *c.* 1947 photograph.

When the Merritt Parkway was fully opened to traffic on September 2, 1940, it became the "Gateway to New England;" traffic analysis showed that 54,163 autos used the Parkway that day. (If placed end to end and using all four lanes, 45,000 vehicles would stretch bumper to bumper over 37 miles from Greenwich to Stratford.) Travelers from New York, New Jersey, and elsewhere included the Parkway in their travel itinerary. To promote tourism, a Parkway information center was erected during 1956 adjacent to the Greenwich Service Station.

Parkway turnarounds were incorporated in the first two sections of road constructed. The turnaround shown above was located one-half mile into Connecticut from the New York state line. Use of the turnarounds was not restricted and as traffic increased on the Parkway, they became highly hazardous. They were removed prior to 1942.

Looking westerly one-quarter mile west of the Greenwich Toll Station, these cars are headed for New York during 1946. At this point in time, the landscaping planted during 1937 has blended with the undisturbed existing natural growth. The two shingle-edge signs look very natural in this setting, which exhibits a pleasing harmony between the works of man and the healing forces of nature. This union of engineering and aesthetics earned the Parkway a title of distinction: "Queen of the Parkways."

As traffic volumes grew heavier, accidents became more frequent and severe. Most commonly, vehicles on the pavement were hit by cars moving along the Parkway. The Parkway's 4-inch-high curbs, intended to carry surface drainage to catch basins and to prevent fill slopes from eroding onto the pavement, caused problems because during emergencies motorists were reluctant to drive over the curbs fearing damage to their vehicles. During 1957, the Connecticut Highway Department (CHD)—shown above—removed much of the curbing in Greenwich and added 2 feet of blacktop.

A completed section of Parkway subbase is shown passing from fill section to cut section through dense woods during the spring of 1937. Grading contracts included the tasks of clearing trees, installing culverts, drilling and blasting rock, and moving earth and rock to fill areas. Topsoil was removed from affected areas and stockpiled for reuse following completion of construction. Fill slopes were seeded and mulched to reduce erosion. Gravel subbase, 12 inches to 24 inches deep, was placed and compacted on the completed subgrade.

This progress photograph taken during late fall of 1935 shows a completed fill and embankment section with completed subbase ready for concrete paving the following spring. Prior to logging and clearing operations, the CHD, Landscape Division moved thousands of healthy trees and shrubs to temporary nurseries. As the Parkway was completed in stages, the cared-for trees and shrubs were transplanted to specific locations on the Parkway in accordance with plans prepared by the highway department.

Although bridle paths were originally included in Parkway planning, a continuous bridle path did not come to pass. In this photograph taken during 1936, two riders and their steeds ride the future Merritt Parkway to Toll Gate Pond. During the construction of the Parkway, the contractor was given permission to excavate gravel from the nearby Byram River, creating an artificial pond. The pond, which is now hidden from view by natural vegetation, received a name when the Greenwich Toll Station was constructed during 1939 at this location.

A light dusting of snow appears on the unopened Parkway and the frozen surface of Toll Gate Pond during January 1938. In this photograph the Parkway environment is largely completed. This location came to serve as a marvelous scenic overlook that enthralled all who drove the Parkway, particularly during the fall foliage season. In the distance is the former driveway to the Nellie Joyce Estate, leading to a dead end but still served by a small, picturesque masonry arch bridge.

This progress photograph taken during 1938 shows a wooden barricade across the completed Parkway that was erected to prevent horseback riders from using the recently graded center park strip. In the distance, the Parkway curves over the Riversville Road Bridge. The curve, designed as 7 degrees and 600 feet in length, is one of the two sharpest on the Parkway. In all, 13 curves were incorporated in the Parkway's design through Greenwich, making the first 8 miles the most dangerous with 558 accidents occurring between 1938 and 1946.

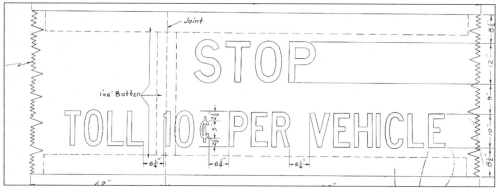

When the legislature passed the Parkway Toll Bill on June 21, 1939, making the Merritt a toll highway, it marked the first time in 15 years that tolls were to be collected on a Connecticut highway or bridge. With passage of the bill, tolls would be collected on the Merritt for 49 years. The intent of the toll collection—misunderstood by many—was to pay for the construction of the Merritt's cousin, the Wilbur Cross Parkway. That road was envisioned to reach Union, Connecticut, and the Massachusetts border.

As the 1939 toll bill was passing through Connecticut's legislature, George Dunkelberger was given the task of designing and building temporary toll booths on the Merritt Parkway in Greenwich. Gathering a group of highway department carpenters at the department's Portland plant, he supervised the construction of prefabricated booths. After being trucked to Greenwich, the booths were erected using wood pins and rubber mallets.

The first 10¢-toll paid on September 21, 1939, is held by Theodore Fleishmann—an unemployed electrical engineer. Between September 21, 1939, and June 30, 1940, $491,850 was collected at the Greenwich Toll Station, reflecting the passage of 4,918,500 vehicles without the Parkway fully opened to Stratford. In the second year of toll collection, traffic was 23 percent heavier than in the corresponding months of the first year. And some drivers, particularly New Yorkers, rebelled by paying in pennies (thereby slowing traffic) and throwing trash on the road.

As the first 10¢-toll is paid by a smiling Theodore Fleishmann to a newly recruited CHD toll collector, a payment was made towards continuing the road beyond Stratford. The Merritt Parkway had become a creative financing maze. Although $15 million in Fairfield County bonds were sold, the bonds were paid by the Highway Fund, a "bank" owned by the CHD with revenues generated by the state-wide gasoline tax. The dimes being collected on the Merritt were used for constructing the Wilbur Cross Parkway.

The temporary toll booths have been completed; those who erected them watch traffic pass through. The Merritt Parkway was the first modern highway to charge tolls and by doing so caused a border war with New York. Westchester County Parkway officials began collecting tolls on their system to snag Connecticut drivers, but they were foiled in this attempt when the New York court system declared the tolls illegal.

The Greenwich Toll Station—shown during the late 1950s—was memorable to many. Passing through the shingled-roofed structure allowed one to pass through a gate into New England. In addition to collecting money, the toll collector served as a good will ambassador for Connecticut, the CHD, and New England. Providing directions and information about r oad conditions, weather, traffic, and the locations of nearby restaurants was part of the job. More than one baby was born at the Greenwich Toll Station and emergency first aid was always available.

This altered scene greeted motorists heading east during July 1977, 37 years after the Greenwich Toll Station was constructed. When the canopy was first created, a flagpole graced the center island with no attachments to the roof other than the signal heads. The single booths were added during 1954 following a series of 1-mile backups and many frayed nerves. As modern amenities were substituted—such as aluminum light poles for wood and metal barrels for slender pipe stanchions and chains—the Parkway aesthetic was modified.

Heavy eastbound traffic from New York approaches the Greenwich Toll Station during the late 1950s. Prior to WW II, the peak times of travel on the Merritt occurred on the weekends. Following WW II, the peak times shifted to include weekday business and commuter trips. During 1939, the Merritt developed a daily average of 13,600 vehicles at Greenwich, compared with 16,400 vehicles on U.S. Route 1 (a reduction from 19,700 vehicles during 1936). By 1956, a daily average of 63,158 vehicles passed through the Greenwich Toll Station.

The permanent toll booths were completed during 1940 and featured Adirondack rustic design. Preliminary designs for the Greenwich and Milford booths were prepared by George Dunkelberger and William Mislick. Since buildings were the responsibility of the public works department, final plans for the toll booths and administration buildings were prepared under its direction. The booth canopies were supported by stripped logs and roofed with hand-split cypress shingles. The administration buildings were rustic too, with exterior walls faced with log corners, split log panels, and square-edge lap siding.

The design of the Parkway occurred in two phases. The first phase, completed by 1940, included the construction of two concrete pavement lanes separated by a center park for traffic in two directions. These were built on the north side of the 300 feet of right-of-way, with phase two to be constructed as a nearly mirror image on the south side when traffic increased. The bottom drainage systems—accounting for 56,320 feet of concrete pipe—were installed at particular elevations to allow for the anticipated extensions of phase two.

The Riversville Road Bridge was constructed by the Lee Construction Co. for $85,240 using WPA Funds. Completed during 1935, it carries the Merritt Parkway over Riversville Road and the east branch of the Byram River. Its Classical style, reflected by balustrading and mock abutment arches, is well suited to the natural environment of rural dirt roads and flowing streams. This bridge is built with simply supported, concrete-encased "I" beams.

The Riversville Road Bridge, shown under construction, hosted a Merritt Parkway groundbreaking ceremony on May 23, 1934. Greenwich First Selectman Oscar Tuthill turned the first shovel full of earth; Schuler Merritt delivered the keynote speech. Merritt said, "We believe it [the Parkway] will be designed and built not alone, or even primarily to afford rapid transit, but to be in itself an object of beauty and to tend to the rest and peace and satisfaction of those who inhabit the country and those who pass through it."

A steel "I" beam is put into place as the "brass" below inspect ongoing work at the Riversville Road Bridge site during 1934. Foundation conditions for bridges on the Merritt were excellent, and prevented settlement under heavy traffic loads. Few bridges required pilings, with the majority bearing on ledge rock at convenient depths. The encased "I"-beam design used on the Riversville Road Bridge was rare; only two other Merritt bridges were constructed in this manner. When grading was completed around the bridge, only two-thirds of the structure was visible.

This is the overpass located approximately 2 miles from the New York state line, crossing the Glenville Water Company stream and hiking path. This 1947 photograph illustrates the narrowing of the center park strip from 22 feet to less than 2 feet at the end of a curved section, thereby reducing the required bridge width by 20 feet. This construction was considered substandard and not repeated at similar overpasses at the eastern end of the Parkway. During later years, this section of Parkway was cited for non-uniform operating conditions.

A rigid-frame bridge located 2 miles from the New York line carries the Merritt over lands belonging to the Glenville Water Company. It was constructed during 1935 at a cost of $38,391. Landscaping of the Merritt was of paramount importance, and the Fairfield County Planning Association provided a beautification subcommittee to work with the Parkway designers. The committee assisted nature in hiding the scars of construction and supplemented native plant life already growing. New slopes adjacent to bridge wing walls were covered with erosion-resistant turf.

In the 1920s and 1930s, it was good engineering practice to run new highways in long straight lines, or "tangents." When it became necessary to change direction, the designer laid out a circular curve, the radius of which he selected to fit the ground with the least construction cost but governed by department policy. The CHD established an official curvature of 7 degrees maximum. When completed, the Parkway included 46 curves ranging from 1.5 degrees to 7 degrees.

This 1938 progress photograph shows a small bridge carrying the Merritt over the west branch of the Byram River. Built during 1935, it is one of four bridges on the Parkway constructed as a concrete arch-deck structure. Located about 3 miles from the New York line, the bridge is one of six designed to carry traffic solely over water. It is 64 feet wide, one of the Parkway's narrowest spans. The cedar trees and shrubs planted in the center were intended to block headlight glare from opposing lanes of traffic.

This image shows the Round Hill Road Underpass looking east with Portland cement concrete pavement in place. The pavement cross section is widened with a narrowed center park strip. This allowed for a shortened bridge span length and increased economy. It was near this location and under a 30-foot elm tree that a time capsule was placed honoring the Parkway landscaping. The time capsule remains in place with the tree removed long ago.

The Round Hill Road Underpass frames a vista of the Leona Helmsley Estate. Constructed during 1935 at a cost of $45,694, the underpass construction with its classic theme draws its beauty from the elegant estate in the distance. This bridge is a reinforced concrete rigid-frame

structure with outstanding workmanship. A careful comparison of the left and right abutments reveals a shorter right abutment designed to match an eventual twin bridge to the right for a future Parkway expansion.

A 1935 view of the Round Hill Road Underpass shows Round Hill Road curving uphill to the right in the distance. Providing a means for riders on horseback to cross the Parkway meant constructing unpaved shoulders on the bridge approaches. Hoof prints and wagon-wheel tracks are visible on the right shoulder. Unknown to many who drive the Parkway and just a mile and a half to the east of this location is a 12-foot-wide concrete tunnel built in 1934 that allows riders to pass under the Parkway.

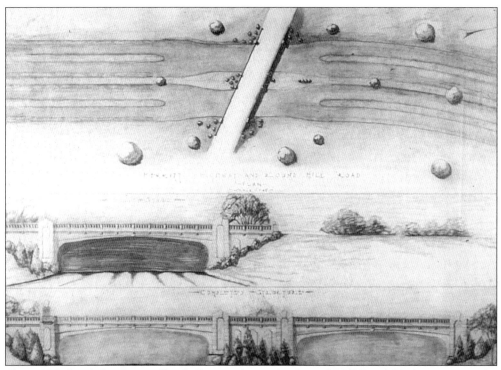

This 1935 sketch by George Dunkelberger shows the Round Hill Road Underpass over the expanded Merritt Highway. It was foreseen by the Merritt's planners and designers that traffic would eventually overwhelm the initial construction completed during 1940. The completion of additional bridges into Manhattan by Robert Moses resulted in the transformation of the Parkway from a pleasure road to a commuter road following WW II.

The Lake Avenue Underpass was designed as a rigid-frame steel structure. Constructed during 1940 and referred to as the "Grapes of Wrath" bridge, it was one of the last bridges built on the Merritt Parkway. The vertical trellises are composed of three separate sections of cast malleable iron, each weighing one thousand pounds. They were cast by Eastern Malleable Iron of Naugatuck with great difficulty due to the ratio of metal between the grapes and the stem.

The Lake Avenue Underpass provides a picturesque contrast to the predominant concrete bridges on the Merritt Parkway. The horizontal trellises below the railing are made of pre-cast concrete. Construction of the bridge was delayed when a shortage of steel developed as war broke out in Europe. No bridge existed at the site when the first 18-mile section of the Parkway was opened on June 29, 1938.

The North Street Underpass was built during 1937 at a cost of $45,782. At the time of its construction, the North Street Underpass was among the five widest bridges on the Parkway. Built as a concrete rigid-frame structure, it is skewed 30 degrees to the Parkway baseline. As a skewed bridge it cost more to build due to its longer length. The North Street Underpass and its sister bridge, the Ponus Street Underpass in New Canaan, are among the nearly one-third of the Parkway bridges designed in the neo-Classical style.

A car approaches the notoriously dangerous curve number 11 about 6 miles from the New York border during 1947. A total of 16 serious accidents occurred here over eight years. During 1950, this one-half-mile section of the Merritt was relocated 100 feet to the north with a 4.5-degree curve in place of the 7-degree curve originally constructed. Moving the Parkway at this location was difficult and costly. Reconstruction required the doubling in length of an 8-by-6-foot concrete box culvert running under the Parkway, making it the road's longest.

The Taconic Road Overpass was completed during 1937 and proved to be a costly project in terms of construction and public relations. The bridge, with an arch span of 55 feet, was one of the most expensive overpasses on the Parkway. Costing $57,018, it was difficult to build and soon after completion suffered a severe crack on the northwest end caused by a shifting of subsoil under the footings. A construction joint that would have accommodated such a shifting was purposely left out to improve the aesthetics. Although not a danger to the safety of the bridge, the crack was seized upon by Robert Hurley in his quest to discredit the CHD while he was commissioner of the rival state public works department.

This photograph, taken for Robert Hurley to discredit State Highway Commissioner John MacDonald, shows a crack in the Taconic Road Overpass on December 14, 1937.

The Parkway landscaping was a tremendous achievement. Of the 2,288 acres of land purchased for the Parkway, 1,354 were devoted to the uniform right-of-way strip that is 300 feet wide, 266 were used for intersections, and 250 were paved. Remaining were 1,370 acres that required landscaping. Foresters working under the direction of landscape architect Thayer Chase planted 47,000 mountain laurels, 11,000 evergreens, and 3,777 dogwoods according to a philosophy called "site setting," which blended the new landscape with the old.

The Stanwich Road Underpass was designed by George Dunkelberger as a concrete rigid-frame structure and built during 1937 at a cost of $30,811. It had a Classical appearance, combining a balustrade parapet wall with a cast-in-place dentil. Its pylons, however, are decorated in an Art Deco theme with bas-relief floral designs providing balance to the approaches. This 1941 photograph reflects how open the Parkway environment was until vegetation became overgrown, a center beam rail was installed, and heavy traffic filled the roadways.

Two

STAMFORD

Waiting for the Merritt Parkway to be completed was a challenge for many drivers. U.S. Route 1 is shown during 1932, having been recently widened from Greenwich to Bridgeport. The Greenwich-Stamford town line is seen in the distance. During peak hours of use, the widened roadway became jammed with local traffic competing with interstate traffic thrown together with a high percentage of slow-moving trucks. The open area to the left was the original location of U.S. Route 1, which was two lanes wide.

Anna Dunkelberger (wife of George) is on the left and George Dunkelberger appears on the right in this photograph. George L. Dunkelberger was born to a Pennsylvania Dutch family and educated at the Drexel Institute in Philadelphia. Trained as an architect and possessing superb artistic abilities, Dunkelberger became the CHD's architect in 1941. He served as site coordinator for the Merritt Parkway bridges and prepared drawings reflecting a wide range of styles stressing variety and visual stimulation.

GEORGE L. DUNKELBERGER

Died January 26, 1960

George L. Dunkelberger of East Madeira Beach, Florida was born on July 9, 1891, the son of the late George S. and Margaret Delaney Dunkelberger.

He was a retired employee of the Connecticut State Board of Education, and an architect with the Connecticut State Highway Department for 17 years where he designed many of the bridges on the Merritt Parkway.

He lived in Wethersfield 35 years before moving to Florida a year ago.

Mr. Dunkelberger was a member of the Connecticut Society of Civil Engineers for 24 years, having been elected in August of 1936.

He is survived by his wife, Mrs. Anna Grise Dunkelberger of Madeira Beach, Florida and several nieces and nephews.

His many friends and associates in Connecticut were grieved at the news of his death, and he will long be remembered by all who knew him.

Prepared by Edgar B. Vinal.

A young lad peers from the open window of the family sedan during 1946 in Stamford while his dad answers questions relating to the origin and destination of their trip, which included the use of the Merritt Parkway. The information from these studies helped determine the postwar travel patterns on the Parkway and the impact of extending the parkway system to Meriden and beyond. Although the Wilbur Cross Parkway was under construction at this time, a temporary connection to U.S. Route 5 was made north of Meriden. The temporary connection became permanent and the parkway design to Union was shelved in favor of enlarging the Berlin Turnpike to four lanes, allowing mixed traffic and improving the route east of the Connecticut River as the Wilbur Cross Highway.

The stone-faced footbridge above was designed by Henry Richardson and constructed during 1881 in the Boston Fens. Considered a masterpiece of public works architecture with its ring stones and band course, it serves as a model for larger bridges built in the Richardsonian Rustic tradition.

Certainly rustic and compatible with its environment, a typical underpass on New York's Westchester County Hutchinson River Parkway lacks the charisma of the Merritt Parkway bridges. Its spirit is Richardsonian and exemplifies the Bronx River Parkway, completed during 1924. The Merritt was designed as a "modern" parkway during the Art Deco era with a theatrical theme intended to relieve the monotony of bridge after bridge presenting the same visual effect. Many people in Fairfield County were dismayed upon hearing that the Merritt bridge facings would be constructed with combinations of ornamental concrete and executed with economy in mind and creativity in spirit.

The Rocky Craig Underpass frames a vista of the Riverbank Road Underpass half a mile to the east during 1938. Constructed during 1937 and costing $26,400, the structure's graceful design is reminiscent of Henry Richardson's footbridge in the Boston Fens. But the Rocky Craig Underpass is more rustic, using uncut fieldstones above the square-cut ring stones of the arch.

The stones, however, are only "skin deep." Beneath the stone facade is a reinforced concrete rigid-frame structure. The stone facing was negotiated during the property acquisition for this section of the Parkway. A very similar structure, the Stockley Bridge, exists in Borrowdale, England, and probably served as the model for the Rocky Craig (Guinea Road) Underpass.

This westerly view from the Riverbank Road Underpass shows the Rocky Craig Underpass in the distance during the early 1950s. The caution sign on the westbound side, placed to warn drivers of construction ahead, was extremely large and a trademark of road construction projects undertaken by the CHD. Each sign displayed two large red dots and a pair of red lanterns, which burned night and day. During the 15 years since this section of the Parkway was opened, the foliage had reached maturity in the center park strip.

A side hill is being excavated by power shovel during 1938 and placed as fill in the foreground. Prior to any construction activity or grading work, trained foresters supervised logging operations to protect all trees not actually in the path of construction. Stumps, dead trees and limbs, underbrush, and general debris were removed and burned to improve the appearance of the future roadside. These labor-intensive activities served the goals of the National Recovery Act and benefited the aesthetic objectives of the Parkway's planners.

Although considered by some to be a model in its day, the Merritt was seen by others as outdated the day construction began. This westerly view from Riverbank Road shows a kinked alignment resulting from two long tangents being connected by a short circular curve. This type of alignment takes place over 84 percent of the Parkway's length and was considered a step backward from the continuous curvature of the New York and Virginia Parkways. To ensure the possible expansion of the Parkway in the future, initial construction took place only on the north side of the 300-foot right-of-way. This confined the initial layout to a 150-foot width, making continuous curvature difficult.

The Riverbank Road Underpass illustrates the use of Art Deco styling. Constructed during 1937 and costing $25,673, the structure's style became a source of criticism. Elizabeth Mock described the bridge as one ". . . whose vulgar ornament is peculiar to our times and easy achievement in this docile material." The intent of the Merritt Parkway bridge design team was to present a pleasing effect in the mind of the *traveler*, not the art critic.

An unfortunate but not unusual event clouded the Parkway's right-of-way acquisition. In the spring of 1937, Attorney General Daley discovered that unduly high prices were being paid for Merritt Parkway land. Following an investigation, a private state purchasing agent was jailed and Commissioner MacDonald resigned. Until 1939, Connecticut lacked the legal right to deny access to a public highway. The state was forced to buy the land that normally would have access and for this reason the acquisition of a 300-foot park strip shown in the photograph during 1950 was a legal device to gain full control of access.

The Wire Mill Road Underpass frames a vista of farmland in the distance. Constructed during 1937 and costing $28,343, its curved wing walls and deep shadowing effects are embellished with balustrading. This bridge reflects George Dunkelberger's belief that highway architecture must incorporate the existing landscape. Its curved wing walls merge with the site contours. Constructed entirely of reinforced concrete as a rigid-frame structure, the Wire Mill Road Underpass is one of the first Parkway structures erected in Stamford.

This view looking up the Rippowam River includes the Parkway's only stone-faced river bridge. During the planning phases of the Parkway, stone-faced bridges were ruled out because of their cost, but the Rippowam River Bridge was constructed as an exception in 1936. Seen only by an adjacent property owner, the stone facing of random ashlar was agreed to by the state after difficult and acrimonious negotiation with a famous stone sculptor, a portion of whose estate was required as a right-of-way. The sculptor died prior to the bridge being completed.

This progress photograph taken during the spring of 1938 shows that this section of the Parkway lacked only topsoil in the center park strip. The concrete pavement was placed in four strips each 13 feet, 8 inches in width. Each block measured 25 feet in length and the four strips shown, each approximately 1,000 feet in length, took four days to place using a paving train riding on the pavement forms. Even though the intended use of the Parkway was for passenger vehicles, the pavement and bridges were designed for much heavier traffic.

The Route 137 North Stamford Avenue Overpass is shown following its completion in 1937 at a cost of $40,889. Griffin reliefs—created by embedding an under-layer of black onyx in a concrete slab—adorn one pylon on each side of the overpass. This overpass is a simple span, steel-framed bridge with an unusual facia beam partially hiding the arched steel girders. A bridge with identical reliefs and built during 1938 in Norwalk carries Grumman Avenue over the Parkway.

This progress photograph of the Parkway was taken during the winter shutdown of 1937-38. The High Ridge Road Overpass is seen in the distance. A wooden platform used for dumping wheelbarrows of stones in trucks is visible to the right. Building the Parkway was a labor-intensive project. Although road construction during the 1930s had become highly mechanized, the fine grading of slopes and park strips was done by hand. Steel dowels are seen protruding from the top right of the pavement sections. The dowels were used to connect concrete park curbing to the pavement surface.

The Newfield Avenue Underpass was built during 1937 at a cost of $25,777. Constructed as a concrete rigid-frame structure and photographed during 1939, this underpass exhibits rhythmic qualities in its Art Deco styling. The beaded pylons lend an air of vertical support, acting as mock suspension towers for the dropped parapet wall. The same theme provides balance to the center span with flanking overlapped panels on the wing walls. On closer examination, quadrants have been incorporated at the vertical intersections of adjoining panels on the parapet wall. Such details were Dunkelberger trademarks for the Parkway bridges.

Following a year of construction, a decision was made to incorporate curb-eye reflectors into the concrete park curbing to delineate the pavement edges (the need for the reflectors became apparent during fog and snow conditions, when the light from headlamps was swallowed by the natural foliage). The lenses became scratched from winter sanding operations, however, and in 1945 cat's-eye reflectors were placed in the dome-top guide-rail posts erected in place of the wooden guide-rail fencing.

As the Merritt's traffic volumes increased before and after a brief lull during WW II—surprising motorists and designers—a fundamental change was affecting Parkway use. To the south in metropolitan New York, master builder Robert Moses had crafted the Triborough Bridge, the Henry Hudson Bridge, and the Bronx Whitestone Bridge between July 1936 and April 1939. Access to New York City by automobile using Westchester's parkway system with connections to the Merritt Parkway using the Hutchinson River Parkway Extension quickly transformed the Merritt into a commuter road with parkway characteristics, shown above during 1950. The Merritt unfortunately became a means for earning a living and making a fortune.

Three
NEW CANAAN

Warren Creamer was educated at Trinity College in Hartford. He was appointed project engineer in charge of all operations on the Merritt Parkway, and during 1931, he established a project residency at the Colonial Building in New Canaan.

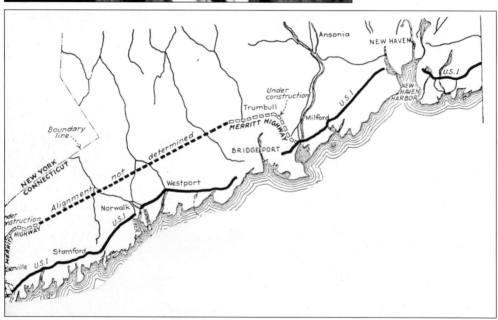

The March 14, 1935 issue of *Engineering New Record* published a composite route map for the Merritt. Construction was underway at both ends, but the CHD was reluctant to release details about the center section until comparative costs were completed for grading, draining, and constructing bridges, and determining what type of road the department could build in the face of strong local sentiment for a parkway design. The CHD, a nearly autonomous public agency, was not interested in constructing a second Bronx River Parkway, but rather an express highway to relieve U.S. Route 1. New standards for highway design were emerging that recognized higher performance and greater speeds from motor vehicles.

Signage associated with the Parkway was in keeping with its understood design goal: aesthetic appearance was as important as engineering. The original five hundred signs on the Parkway were constructed of wood with "shingled" edges. The sign faces were covered with green reflexite and lettered with white gothic characters. This unique signage, which spoke directly to the Parkway user, intensified the Parkway mystique. During 1941, Montclair, New Jersey, and Hagerstown, Maryland, were granted permission by the CHD to use the same design in their municipalities.

A smoker enters traffic heading westbound toward Ponus Ridge during 1951. Forty-three years earlier, the first parkway was constructed on Long Island. William Vanderbilt Jr. organized the Long Island Motor Parkway Company, which built a 45-mile motor road on private right-of-way as a race course for the Vanderbilt Cup. Opened on October 10, 1908, it was one of the first engineered roads in the world to have super-elevated, or banked, curves. Its importance, however, was the relationship of the roadway to its surrounding park-like environment: the American "parkway" was born.

The Ponus Street Underpass was built during 1937 at a cost of $24,167. Constructed as a concrete rigid-frame structure, the underpass was enhanced by George Dunkelberger with mock Quoin stones cast in concrete at the abutment pylons. He included a sense of continuity with the central arch flanked by smaller span arches on each side. This structure is typical of George

Dunkelberger's design technique, which adopted elements of the architectural styles of the 1920s and 30s. His goal was to please the driving public and remain within the economic realities of the Parkway budget. The Ponus Street Underpass suffered severe corrosion and was reconstructed during 1970.

As planning the Parkway led to its design, the CHD staff engineers looked elsewhere for ideas and principles. They were familiar with the earlier parkways, particularly those in Westchester County, New York, built as commuter arteries to augment parallel railroad commuter lines. But Westchester's parkways were run for the most part in valleys and on flat lands. The Merritt's planned alignment was at right angles or transverse to the valleys, particularly between Greenwich and Trumbull. Its construction was limited to 150 feet of the 300 feet purchased.

The New Canaan branch of the New York, New Haven, and Hartford Railroad is shown overpassing the partially constructed Parkway at Talmadge Hill. Prior to the bridge construction in 1937, a "shoo-fly" was installed to route trains around the site. In this photograph, the railroad bridge frames the Route 106 Old Stamford Road Overpass (also constructed during 1937). The railroad bridge was designed by the railroad and the CHD. Built as a rigid-frame concrete structure, the bridge is presently owned and maintained by the Metro-North Commuter Railroad.

This 1938 view looking east with the Lapham Road Underpass near the crest of the hill was taken during the winter shutdown period. Two lanes of eastbound Parkway stretch into the distance while the westbound lanes remain unfinished. A small pipeline is seen in the center park. Extending the length of the Parkway, it provided water to the paving train and for curing the concrete pavement. The upper left cleared area was a portion of Waveny, the Lapham Estate that became Waveny Park. Its open character indicates its previous use as farmland.

With his steam shovel providing a barrier against flying rocks, the engineer watches a dynamite blast disintegrate a section of rock ledge in New Canaan near Lapham Road during 1936. Techniques and equipment developed during WW I revolutionized the road-building industry, with much surplus equipment being used through the 1930s. Blasting techniques on the Parkway project included drilling blast holes using compressed air with holes spaced 5 feet apart. The heavier blasts included 150 holes and 2,000 pounds of dynamite.

This 1936 progress photograph shows a steam shovel loading blasted rock into dump trucks. The hose provided water to the steam boiler. Each steam shovel was operated by two men—one who loaded the trucks and another who fired the boiler and lubricated moving parts. A total of 5,478,621 cubic yards of earth and rock was excavated for the Merritt Parkway. Of this total, over 2,394,000 cubic yards was rock, which placed the Parkway well up among the large rock-grading projects for road building in New England.

This 1950 view from the Lapham Road Underpass shows Ponus Ridge to the west. This section of the Parkway passes through 60 acres of property purchased from the Lapham family, early investors in The Texas Co. (Texaco). A condition of the sale was the construction of earth berms to shield the remaining estate from noise and headlight glare. We see here that two sections of the center park strip are being narrowed. This treatment on earlier sections of the Parkway led to the pinched-bridge controversy between two state commissioners.

The Lapham Avenue Underpass was constructed during 1937 for $23,809, one of the least expensive bridges on the Parkway. Built at a 90-degree angle to the Parkway centerline—a rarity for the Merritt bridges—the Lapham Avenue Underpass is a conservative, concrete rigid-frame structure built during the Art Deco era. Many details used on the Parkway bridges were accentuated so that a tourist could pause and see something more in character and style than the common concrete bridge, an activity acceptable with slower speeds and less traffic.

During the course of constructing the Parkway, numerous compromises were made following intense negotiations over property acquisition. The oak tree shown in this 1937 photograph was a favorite of the Lapham family and was included in the 60-acre parcel of their Waveny estate sold to the state. With the Parkway's alignment already determined and its geometry calculated on two hundred-scale layout sheets, a dilemma arose over the fate of the tree. Through the efforts of the Lapham family and the New Canaan Garden Club, the tree was left intact.

Using trick photography to exaggerate the jog around the oak, Hurley made the road appear dangerously near the tree. MacDonald dispatched his own photographer, and both camera angles were printed in a Bridgeport newspaper. Governor Wilbur Cross entered the fray and was driven past the aging oak twice. He decided that if the tree were trimmed properly, it would be less of a menace. The tree was trimmed and by June of 1938, when the Parkway was partially opened, was in distress with a third of its limbs dead or cut off.

In an attempt to preserve the oak, a stone retaining wall was constructed to contain it and retain the 3 feet of roadway fill. Damage to the tree's root system was minimized with special backfill spread over the roots during construction. The efforts to save the oak tree were in keeping with the wishes of the Lapham's grandmother. Bent on discrediting John MacDonald, Robert Hurley declared the tree a safety hazard and set out to prove it.

During the Parkway's first year of operation, 2.5 million cars passed the Lapham oak without incident. Until August 7, 1939, the Parkway was fatality free. But on this date during early morning darkness, J.V. Picone of Brooklyn, New York, falling asleep at the wheel, smashed into the Lapham oak. Passenger Joseph Picone was killed and on January 30, 1940, the Lapham oak was removed. Later, the pavement was widened and the opposite center curbing straightened at the former tree location.

When grading and draining were completed for a section of the Parkway, a subsequent contract was let for pavement construction. Shown above is a contingent from the Connecticut Society of Civil Engineers inspecting the laying of concrete pavement on September 30, 1937, in New Canaan. Prior to actually placing the concrete, workers installed sturdy steel side rails for the mechanized paving train at exact line and grade for a distance of 1,000 feet. In all, 13 major paving projects were established to construct 37 miles of four-lane concrete Parkway.

The Darien Road Underpass was built during 1937 at a cost of $32,935. Constructed as a concrete rigid-frame structure and photographed during 1939, this underpass is currently carrying South Avenue (Route 124) over the Parkway. It is an outstanding example of Art Deco architecture and is in the first group of bridges reflecting George Dunkelberger's talents. Like its sister bridge at Newfield Avenue in Stamford, the Darien Road Underpass exhibits a rhythmic appearance with overlapping panels on the parapets, pylons, and interior abutment walls.

Following a large number of requests for service stations on the Parkway during late 1938, a design committee consisting of the Hon. Albert Lavery, Judge H. Allyn Barton, and Highway Commissioner Cox (MacDonald's successor) was appointed to recommend suitable sites and appropriate architecture for the stations. Three sites were chosen in Greenwich, New Canaan, and Fairfield for Colonial style facilities. The design chosen was intended to reflect the quiet demeanor of the typical New England village to which many Merritt travelers would be heading.

George Dunkelberger is most remembered for his role as the Merritt Parkway bridge architect. His design talents are also reflected in the unique New Canaan gas stations and the elegant Parkway maintenance building adjacent to the westbound gas station. Originally designed to serve as a headquarters for Parkway operations from Greenwich to Union, the building is constructed of red brick with a segmented glass circular window, gable-ended roofs, and arched entrance.

As planning for the Merritt progressed to the design stage, an issue important to many people was bridge architecture. The CHD was well versed in bridge design by 1934. Its bridge design section, founded in 1915 and having completed two challenging projects, was well equipped with creative individuals to design any structure for the Merritt Parkway. Shown above is the White Oak Shade Road Underpass, completed during 1938 at a cost of $30,563.

In light of the high-class residential character of Fairfield County and the feelings of landowners in places like Greenwich, Greenfield Hill, and Sport Hill, the CHD viewed the construction of the Parkway as an opportunity and incorporated the principles of roadside development, pushing aside vestiges of the City Beautiful Movement. By the time construction stopped on the Parkway during 1940, the CHD was already 45 years old and regarded as a progressive, highly professional, and self-financed organization unlike any other state agency.

The Marvin Ridge Road Underpass (formerly Weed Avenue) frames a vista of the Parkway during 1940. Constructed during 1938 at a cost of $25,976, it reflects the Classical Wedgwood style with a sense of balance between the pair of niched white urns. The bridge was a favorite of Dunkelberger and he used it as an example of design blended perfectly with its location. Dunkelberger's skill included choosing an appropriate design not only for those driving the Parkway, but for those affected by the Parkway as well.

Four

NORWALK

Although U.S. Route 1 through Norwalk had been widened during the late 1920s, its efficiency for handling large volumes of traffic was reduced due to limited control of vehicles entering, leaving, and turning on the roadway. Shown above during 1932 are the absence of a painted center line, a lack of curbing to guide traffic through curb cuts and to control water, the excessive use of billboards, and haphazard land use, all contributing to Route 1's status as a substandard arterial route. The construction of an exclusive road to carry trucks between Bridgeport and New York was studied during 1922 and the idea was discarded because of high cost and excessive impact to shoreline property.

A solution to the traffic problems on U.S. Route 1 made good headlines during 1922, but left a bad impression on Connecticut legislators faced with the ire of property owners along the proposed route between Bridgeport and the New York state line.

A stretch of U.S. Route 1 between Greenwich and New Haven is shown being widened to four lanes. The business on the left was characteristic for the 1925-30 era. The activity on this busy road contributed to an impression of "traffic which brought in the backwash from the cities, leaving a trail of shoddy hot dog stands, dirty filling stations, dance pavilions, and tawdry bungalows" across Fairfield County.

Motorists driving a road like the Merritt Parkway were expected to adjust their speeds to the varying radii, and on the sharper curves safe speeds might be considerably lower than the posted speed limit. When the Merritt Parkway was first opened to traffic on June 29, 1938, the speed limit was 45 m.p.h.; on June 19, 1939, it was 50 m.p.h.; on January 9, 1942, 40 m.p.h.; on October 7, 1942, 35 m.p.h.; on May 9, 1944, 40 m.p.h.; on April 1, 1946, 50 m.p.h.; and on January 1, 1945, 55 m.p.h.

Among the most notable bridges on the Parkway is the Comstock Hill Road Underpass. Constructed during 1938 and costing $27,074, this structure was designed by the CHD as were all of the Parkway structures; however, this design benefited from the collaboration of father and son sculptors Febo and Edward Ferrari. Using waste molds of plaster of Paris cast from

actual, full-scale clay models, the concrete was poured into the abutment form work. Following 30 days of curing and covering with dampened blankets, the concrete and plaster molds were exposed. The plaster was then chipped away and wasted, exposing the relief sculptures of the Native American by Febo Ferrari and the pilgrim by Edward Ferrari.

The waste-mold technique was not uncommon in the 1930s. It was used in the creation of bas-relief images for Rockefeller Center in New York and government buildings in the Midwest. But its use in highway architecture was not common until ornamental facings for the Merritt Parkway were required to cover its rigid-frame bridges.

The waste-mold technique required great care by skilled workers, who had to avoid chipping the concrete relief while the plaster waste mold was being removed one chunk at a time using hammer and chisel. Both Native American and pilgrim were fitting observers of traffic entering and leaving New England.

On the rainy night of October 16, 1955, during a hurricane, a motorist reported something wrong with the Parkway pavement near Silvermine Avenue in Norwalk. The Parkway State Police soon found out why; the roadway was collapsing over the Silvermine River. For the first time since its 1940 opening, the Merritt Parkway was closed to through traffic.

The Silvermine River Bridge, constructed during 1938, was built as a rigid-frame concrete arch, 40 feet wide and 18 feet high. It extended 100 feet under the Parkway. During the hurricane flooding, the stream bed dropped several feet under the arch footings, causing the entire structure to fail along with the roadway above it. The 17-year-old arch was estimated to have passed a flood five times the mean annual flood of the Silvermine River.

This image depicts the events that transpired on the morning of October 19, 1955. Working around the clock, men and machines tirelessly prepared the site for the construction of military Bailey Bridges for westbound traffic and improvised steel-girder wood-deck bridges for eastbound traffic. Peter Racskowski (in the white jumpsuit), who served during WW II as an officer in the Army Corps of Engineers, supervises the erection of the temporary bridges as an engineer for the CHD.

The Silvermine River Bridge was one of six bridges designed to carry the Parkway over rivers of varying widths. With the exceptions of the Saugatuck and Rippowam River Bridges, each of the river bridges utilized standardized design elements common to river crossings throughout the state.

On the morning of October 19, 1955, we look eastbound as the first section of the WW II-era Bailey Bridge is set into place. Three towering truck cranes were pressed into service following a difficult trip over a road designed for cars. Meanwhile, with the Parkway closed to traffic around Norwalk, 50,000 cars a day jammed U.S. Route 1 and detour roads, reminiscent of the pre-Parkway era.

The afternoon of October 19, 1955, saw steady progress, with two Bailey Bridges being constructed for westbound traffic. Each bridge included hundreds of parts and sections to be assembled by hand in exact sequence. Reopening the Parkway was extremely important, considering the fact that widespread damage to other roads and bridges in Fairfield County was disrupting traffic entering and leaving New York.

The morning of October 20, 1955, saw the first wood-deck bridge on the Merritt Parkway. Being unable to locate additional Bailey Bridges for the eastbound lanes, the CHD was forced to employ a creative solution. Steel beams about to be used on the nearby Connecticut Turnpike bridges were "borrowed" for temporary use on the Merritt Parkway. Square timbers were placed on the steel beams to create a temporary bridge.

On the afternoon of October 20, 1955, the Merritt Parkway was reopened in the westbound direction while work continued on the improvised eastbound timber-deck bridge. The Comstock Hill Road Bridge is visible in the distance. Two years later, a modern, three-span replacement bridge was constructed at this location with double the waterway area of the original arch bridge.

This October 13, 1939 aerial view shows the Merritt Parkway/U.S. Route 7 interchange. Although not geometrically perfect, the ramp layout became Connecticut's first cloverleaf design with inner and outer loops designated for one-way traffic, avoiding a crossover condition on U.S. Route 7. The U.S. Route 7 Overpass was of unique design, with an open well in the center park strip and abutments faced with fieldstone. This interchange reflected the emerging expressway standards being adopted by the American Association of State Highway Officials (AASHO), of which Connecticut was a member.

The 1938 West Rocks Road Underpass is one of the longest underpasses on the Parkway at 184 feet. When constructed, it was tinted a light green, much of which has disappeared through overpainting and weathering. This structure has exposed steel girders and is what George Dunkelberger referred to as a functional structure expressing itself by the components used in its construction. The Parkway bridges as well as the roadway and park have been referred to as the marriage of engineering with aesthetics. Occasionally, the engineering considerations dominate.

The 1938 East Rocks Road Underpass is a concrete rigid-frame structure with simple lines reflecting the Art Deco era. Bas-relief floral designs appear on the fluted pylons, providing continuity between the structure and the Parkway's landscape. The Connecticut State Seal, also in bas relief, graces the center of the span. Although only 12 years old when this photograph was taken, the arch bears signs of efflorescence. This condition, resulting from alkali bleeding from the concrete, is caused by water penetrating the surface—a chronic problem for the Merritt's bridges.

The Grumman Avenue Underpass frames a vista of 1998 reality. Constructed during 1938, this underpass is very similar to the 1937 North Stamford Avenue Overpass in Stamford. Both bridges contain griffins as decorative elements on their abutment pylons. A careful examination of the Merritt bridges reveals many similarities between underpasses and overpasses often miles apart. The griffins on the Grumman Avenue Underpass are reliefs created by the embedding of an underlayer of black onyx in the concrete slab.

A scene envisioned by the Parkway planners and designers greets travelers passing through Connecticut on the Merritt. Tastefully designed landscaping and carefully maintained grass, trees, and shrubs are necessary to provide a park-like environment. This view looking easterly from the Grumman Avenue Underpass during 1949 shows the absence of a center median beam rail, minimal signs, unobtrusive drainage structures, and limited heavy traffic. George Gunther referred to the Merritt as "the most beautiful highway in the U.S.A."

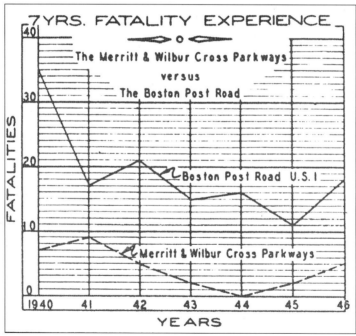

The Merritt Parkway only took a few years to become obsolete as a pleasure road. During 1940, the Parkway exceeded its design capacity in 50 separate instances, as measured at the Greenwich Toll Station. From 1940 to 1950, Fairfield County's population grew by 20 percent; much of this growth followed WW II. Pleasure driving became commuter driving with peak hours growing longer. By 1976, the average daily traffic count reached 33,000 vehicles. By 1988, more than 50,000 cars a day traveled between Stamford and New Canaan.

Five

WESTPORT

This 1930 photograph taken for the Connecticut Motor Vehicles Department shows U.S. Route 1 passing through Westport during off-peak hours. The dark-stained concrete pavement reveals heavy traffic usage, supporting the need for the planned parallel route referred to during 1930 as U.S. Route 1A. This proposed artery was constructed as the non-commercial Merritt Parkway.

A survey party works in the vicinity of Westport. From left to right are as follows: "Bob" Marshall (instrument man), Jack Conaty (chief), and Ed Dolan and Fred Germond (rodmen). The Merritt Parkway project was divided into sections approximately 7 miles in length, with each section requiring extensive surveying for use by design teams. Five survey teams ran line, set benchmarks, took cross sections, recorded topography, and established property boundaries. Referred to as "Sons of Martha," the surveyors trudged through uncharted paths in severe weather.

The 1939 Newton Avenue Underpass is thought by many to be faced with stone. Actually, the facing material is composed of cast concrete. The same material was used for facing buildings in a procedure well known to Dunkelberger, who designed apartment buildings prior to joining the CHD design staff. The texture was obtained by roughening the surface of the concrete prior to its setting and spraying chemicals on the surface to produce the finish. This bridge was designed with a constant-width center park strip to counter Robert Hurley's criticisms.

The 1939 Clinton Avenue Underpass was unusual with its turreted abutments and exposed, riveted facia girder. Built by the Mariani Construction Co., the underpass embodies a military consciousness and was originally proposed for Newtown Avenue in Westport. Instead, a masonry styled underpass was constructed at Newtown Avenue over a wider center park strip. George Dunkelberger visited the Clinton Avenue Underpass twice to check on reports of lime bleeding through the precast concrete panels; on the second visit he discovered the concrete portions of the bridge covered with white frost.

With the factories of war sending plumes of smoke over Bridgeport on the horizon, a convoy heads west on the Parkway. George Dunkelberger drew this sketch following the war department's request to use the Parkway for convoys and commercial vehicles carrying explosives after a wartime "coastal blackout" directive. A temporary toll station was placed at the CHD New Canaan Maintenance Yard adjacent to the Parkway at Darian Road to collect tolls from the commercial trucks. This system remained in effect from June 15, 1943, to August 18, 1945.

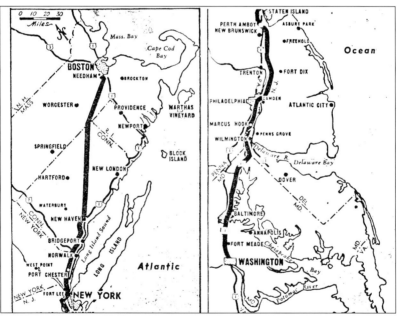

A little-noticed proposal was promulgated to build a new road from Boston to Washington during the war. Referred to as the 7-State Highway, the road's role as a defense highway was emphasized by New Jersey Highway Commissioner E. Donald Sterner on February 26, 1942. The road's planned route through Connecticut included the remaining 150-foot right-of-way for the Merritt Parkway plus additional land. Commissioner MacDonald was in favor of the 7-State, but the project did not receive the required Priority and Reference Rating needed for its continued design.

The North Avenue Underpass was designed with a functional, but decorative appearance. Built during 1939 amid the waning days of the Art Deco era, its inner shell of rebar reinforced concrete is contrasted with the crenellations of the parapet and abutment sidewalls. It was lauded by many as a fine example of Art Deco styling and criticized by others who feel the style is not appropriate in Colonial New England. The bridge exhibits a variety of colors through the use of Wisconsin black onyx and Swedish emerald pearl in layered graffito work on the field-installed precast concrete panels.

The building of the Merritt Parkway became a subject for the WPA artists' and writers' project. A 1937 watercolor painting by Howard Heath depicts workers constructing a typical Merritt Parkway underpass. Clearly shown are the hook bars that provided reinforcing for the rigid-frame construction. During the six-year period of Parkway construction, in excess of three thousand people were employed and 592,313 barrels of Portland cement were mixed to build it.

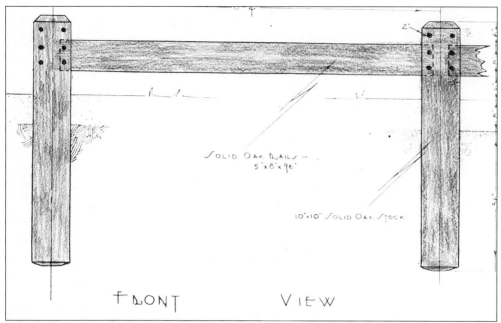

SOLID OAK RAILS —
5"x8"x96"

10"x10" SOLID OAK STOCK

FRONT   VIEW

A long-remembered feature of the Merritt Parkway is the wooden guide rail fencing originally placed to warn motorists of roadside hazards such as steep slopes and open water courses. On steep embankments, hand-hewn oak double-rail guide fences were installed. On flat slopes, a lower, single-rail fence outlined the tops of hills. The damp, harsh environment meant that the joints and dowels of the fences were deteriorating by 1950. During 1954-1956, the rustic wood fences were replaced with two cable guide railings fastened to domed posts.

WOODEN GUIDE RAIL FENCE

ALL LUMBER TO BE SOUND, SQUARE EDGED OAK, DIMENSIONS DRESSED.
ALL POSTS SHALL BE SQUARE AND SET ON 8'-4" CENTERS. (DOUBLE RAIL POSTS 10"x10"x80",
    SINGLE RAIL POSTS 10"x10"x64) 2½" BEVEL FACES AT TOP; ADZED ON FACE AND TWO SIDES.
RAILS SHALL BE 5"x8"x96", ADZED ON TOP AND FACE.
DOWEL PINS SHALL BE 1" DIAMETER; PROJECT 1" BEYOND FACE OF POST; AND INSET INTO RAIL
    NOT LESS THAN ½".
CENTER LINE OF DOWEL PINS SHALL BE 2" FROM EDGE OF POSTS AND INSET INTO RAIL 2" FROM
    TOP AND BOTTOM EDGE OF RAIL.
SIDES OF POSTS TO BE DRILLED AND NOTCHED AT LEAST 3" TO ALLOW FULL INSET OF RAILS.
BOLTS SHALL BE ¼" GALVANIZED.
NO NAILS SHALL BE USED.
ALL SURFACES SHALL BE TREATED WITH ONE APPLICATION OF CARBOSOTA, THE COLOR TO BE
    SELECTED BY THE ENGINEER.
ALL RAILS AND POSTS TO BE SET TO GRADES AND LINES GIVEN BY THE ENGINEER.
PAYMENT WILL BE MADE AT THE CONTRACT UNIT PRICE PER LINEAR FOOT FOR WOODEN GUIDE
    RAIL FENCE COMPLETE IN PLACE ACCORDING TO TYPE –

The specifications for wooden rail fencing are shown in George Dunkelberger's freehand architectural style. The original wood fencing was very aesthetic and complemented the shingle-edge signing and Adirondack style architecture of the Parkway toll stations. The wooden guide rail, however, did little to control errant fast-moving vehicles, and in many cases became a fixed object that penetrated the fronts of vehicles. The removal of the wooden guide rail fencing was the first of many changes to the Parkway's original design.

Six
FAIRFIELD

This 1930 scene shows the widened Boston Post Road passing through Fairfield four years after being designated as U.S. Route 1. Trolley-car tracks are visible in the distance. The white center line prohibits left turns to the intersecting road on the right. The designation of U.S. 1, U.S. 5, U.S. 6, and U.S. 7 in Connecticut during 1926 introduced continuous interstate routes to the State. Fairfield was among the first towns in Connecticut to reap the benefits of improved traffic flow on U.S. 1 prior to the Merritt Parkway.

This 1949 view taken by a CHD photographer captures a panorama of Parkway traffic from the Park Avenue Bridge location. Vintage cars include Packard, Nash, Ford, Dodge, Buick, Chevrolet, and Studebaker. Quality workmanship was a tenet of the Parkway project, which made good use of skilled artisans normally employed in the building trades but short of work during the Depression era. Their talents were depended upon for constructing the Parkway bridges. Creating the sharp and crisp lines true to form and design required workmanship of the highest order.

84

The Merwins Lane Underpass was constructed during 1940 with the secondary purpose of carrying a bridle path over the Parkway. Its intricate design was intended to be enjoyed at a slow pace, either as a walker or rider. As a structure, Merwins Lane is not imposing; however, as a piece of art, Merwins Lane is impressive. George Dunkelberger was fond of all creatures, large and small. He provided shelves on the abutments to hold large concrete butterflies, a theme repeated in the railing castings. The same castings include spider webs and large bulbous spiders peering at passing traffic. A close examination of the railings also reveals a horse and rider, echoing the original intention of carrying a bridle path across the bridge.

A clay model of the larger Merwins Lane butterfly is shown at right. The concrete butterflies clinging to the Merwins Lane Underpass were drawn by George Dunkelberger and prior to being cast in concrete were molded in clay by Edward Ferrari.

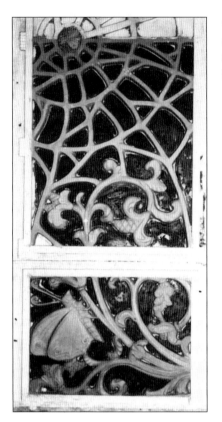

Two plaster castings of the Merwins Lane Underpass railing are shown with the butterfly to the left and spider web to the right. The railing was originally galvanized to reflect the sunlight.

The actual metal casting of the spider clings to the Merwins Lane Underpass railing during 1965.

A clay model of the Merwins Lane railing spider sits on sculptor Ferrari's workbench, sharing space with his shoes and a set of George Dunkelberger's detail drawings for the bridge.

The Redding Road Underpass deserves mention for its simplicity. Constructed during 1939, its deeply grooved abutment faces create a pleasing shadow effect as the sun's rays pass across the surface. A curious feature of this underpass is the differing pylon arrangement on either side of the arch. Most of the Parkway underpasses are equally balanced with identical pylons on each side of their arches. It may well be that this underpass was designed to connect physically with an identical underpass when the Parkway was to be expanded. The right-hand abutment would become the center pier of an extended bridge.

The Congress Street Underpass was constructed during 1938 and photographed during 1946. Ivy has partially hidden the abutment pylons of the Art Deco-styled bridge. After eight years of being exposed to traffic fumes and air pollution, the superstructure is very clean with minimal streaking from pollutants. Dunkelberger designed the Merritt's concrete bridges with a constant vigilance toward eliminating the wash of vertical surfaces from rainwater spilling over from flat surfaces. This was accomplished by designing the flat surfaces to pitch inward, thereby draining the water away from the decorative facade. He introduced drips to cut the flow of water that did reach the vertical surfaces.

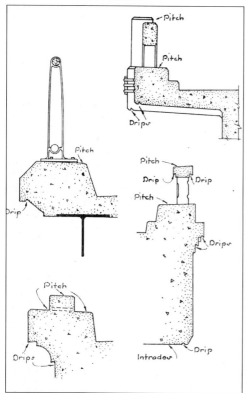

George Dunkelberger's design details for controlling sheet flow and staining on vertical concrete surfaces are shown above. These details were included in the final design plans for the Merritt Parkway bridges.

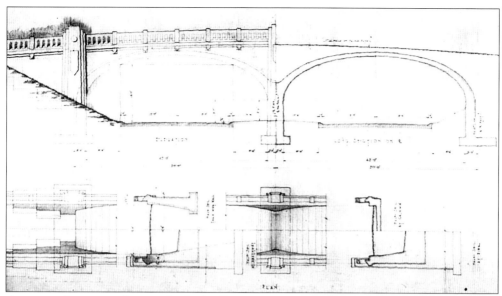

An original concept drawing by Leslie Sumner, engineer of bridges for the CHD, shows a standard plan for bridle-path underpasses on the Merritt Parkway. Adorned with gladiator decor and only 12 feet in width, these underpasses were planned at locations where a continuous bridle path would cross the Parkway. However, liability considerations and the reluctance of the CHD to maintain a continuous bridle path eliminated the bridle path underpasses. Instead, designs were executed for enlarged bridle-path concrete tunnels to pass under the Parkway, with one constructed in Greenwich and another planned in Fairfield.

A collage of Merritt Parkway images forms the January 1947 cover of *Cuts and Fills*, the CHD's monthly magazine. Central to the collage is the owl found in bas relief on the Hillside Road Overpass in Fairfield. Conjecture about the inspiration for the owl has included consideration of George Dunkelberger's training at Drexel Institute in Philadelphia and his possible interest in the students at nearby Bryn Mawr College. The owl is Bryn Mawr's mascot.

One of three celebration bridges on the Parkway, the 1939 Burr Street Underpass incorporates a swing from Classical to Art Deco styling. It also reflects the use of civilized allusion in a public expression of architecture. The decorations include free-hanging triglyphs and classical parapets, elements that point to a world larger than the Parkway environment and do not necessarily appeal to the masses. Mounted on each pylon is a reverse-mold bas relief fashioned by Edward Ferrari to commemorate the workers who built the Parkway.

As the party chief studies a set of plans for the Parkway, his instrument man peers through a transit to pick up a point in the distance. Between them a rodman waits to cut foliage interfering with the sight line. When George Dunkelberger sketched this scene of CHD surveyors, he dramatized the team effort necessary to establish a system of controls to concisely locate the new Parkway. Sculptor Edward Ferrari captured the drama with his bas reliefs on the pylons of the Burr Street Underpass.

This 1954 view of the Parkway in Fairfield shows a bridle path at the foot of the roadway embankment. With many bridle paths crossing the Parkway right-of-way prior to construction, planners envisioned a continuous bridle path parallel to the road. Such a plan was pleasing to the many estate owners through whose properties the Parkway would pass. To carry the bridle path over the Parkway at selected locations, a special 12-foot-wide arch bridge was designed. Although vague in scope and not well maintained, a bridle path did exist without the special bridges.

This westerly 1947 view of the Parkway shows the road's curvilinear alignment extending nearly 1.5 miles to the west. The gradient in the foreground is 7 percent, which is one out of four locations on the Parkway that is greater than 6.9 percent. The Parkway passes Cricker Brook, continues over Black Rock Turnpike, and ascends a 6-percent grade to the Burr Street Underpass. In the foreground, the Parkway passes through a heavy rock cut requiring extensive drilling and blasting. The spoil from the cut was transported down grade and used in the large fill over Cricker Brook.

With their options limited because of topography and a limited construction area of 150 feet, the Merritt's designers adopted a policy of short curves and long tangents; subsequent parkways were built with long curves and short tangents. Connecticut paid a price for not utilizing the entire right-of-way for initial construction. When completed, the Merritt Parkway was a transitional road with parkway characteristics combined with high-speed freeway design. Although designed for 45-m.p.h. travel, the Parkway currently handles speeds of over 60 m.p.h.

The Morehouse Highway Underpass is shown during 1998, 59 years after its 1939 construction completion. Its design reflects a unique engineering problem at the site. Morehouse Highway is on a descending grade from right to left, requiring an underpass with varying elevation. George Dunkelberger adopted a stepped design from right to left, echoing Frank Lloyd Wright's 1924 Ennis House, which makes use of stepped blocks.

This 1947 view shows the Fairfield service stations on each side of the Parkway. Design and construction of the service stations, with the exception of the ones at New Canaan, was undertaken by the state public works department. Considerable effort was made to blend the original stations and pump areas into the Parkway's environment. During 1948-49 the stations' three emergency service cars responded to 4,300 calls for help. The three stations sold 5 million gallons of gasoline and 1,700,000 persons used the stations' restrooms.

The 1936 Sport Hill Road Underpass was constructed for $33,285. A concrete rigid-frame structure, this bridge is skewed 20 degrees to the Parkway centerline. Recessed niches in the abutment pylons provide a decorative contrast to the plain concrete surfaces of the arch and wingwalls. This bridge serves an interchange originally designed as a full cloverleaf but constructed with three traffic loops. Parkway land use in the area includes the interchange and, just to the south, the Fairfield service stations built during 1941. A Parkway restaurant designed for this area was never built.

Since 1913, when the first trunk line highway map for Connecticut was approved by the state legislature, the CHD has issued an annual tourist map for public use. For the first time since the Merritt Parkway was fully opened during 1940, a scene of the Parkway was featured on the 1946 tourist map along with an artist's rendition of Connecticut's "New England Portal."

Signs warning of construction work on the Merritt were billboard size—6 feet by 8 feet—and very obvious to the motorist. Constructed of matched boards painted white and lettered in black with two large red dots, they were designed to deliver a visual impact and were used until 1960 when a much smaller version was adopted.

Seven

TRUMBULL

The Park Avenue Underpass frames a vista of the Fairfield town line to the west as autos descend the 6-percent grade toward Sport Hill Road. Constructed during 1940, this structure was one of three that was modified to allow for a widened park strip following the pinched bridge criticisms of public works Commissioner Robert Hurley. The Park Avenue Underpass is among the more prominent on the Parkway and resembles the Rialto Bridge over Venice's Grand Canal. Designed by George Dunkelberger with a neo-Gothic theme, the structure

exhibits an elegance reflecting New York City's Park Avenue in the regional sense and Bridgeport's Park Avenue in the local sense. Its neo-Gothic theme is complemented with artificial waterspouts and rifle slits on the parapets. Each abutment pylon exhibits the Trumbull Town Seal in reverse-mold bas relief. Unlike most bridges on the Parkway, the Park Avenue Underpass is a concrete-arch deck design, one of four structures built on the Merritt allowing for a thin arch section pleasing to the eye and elegant in appearance.

This 1947 view of the Parkway shows the Park Avenue Underpass peeking through the foliage as cars descend the grade toward the Route 59 Underpass. The significance of the Merritt Parkway was documented during a 1992 study by a seven-member team of experts from the Historic American Buildings Survey/Historic American Engineering Record (HABS/HAER), a division of the National Park Service. Their unbiased architectural drawings, photographs, and written data were placed on file with the Library of Congress to serve as a permanent record of the Parkway's significance.

Upon completion of the Merritt, George Dunkelberger was asked to sketch a bird's-eye view of a Parkway scene he particularly enjoyed. He chose the Park Avenue Underpass in Trumbull with the Sport Hill Road Underpass and Morehouse Highway Underpass in the distance. The sketch, with Park Avenue as a focal point, was used on the cover of the 1940 highway Commissioner's "Biennial Report." The Park Avenue Underpass was also used to symbolize the Parkway on the state's 125th anniversary plate, issued during 1943.

The early decision to reduce the span length of underpasses on the Parkway to save money required narrowed center-park widths at underpass locations. Seizing a political opportunity to discredit the state highway department and frustrated at being unable to absorb the department into his own public works agency, Robert Hurley did his best to criticize the Parkway's engineering. He criticized various elements of the Parkway, one of which was the center-park pinch effect at underpasses. Governor Cross sought the expertise and third-party advice of the respected Charles Bennett, a Yale engineering graduate and former highway Commissioner. As Johnny Anderson's cartoon of the time depicts, the three criticized bridges were balanced with three updated and not yet constructed bridges using Bennett's expertise.

Referred to as the "Texaco Bridge," the Plattsville Road Underpass was constructed during 1939, when Plattsville Road was named Chestnut Hill Road. Industrial designer Walter Dorwin Teague was contracted by Texaco during 1937 to develop a new set of service station designs. Teague believed that "every man who plans the shape and line and color of an object—whether it is a painting, statue, chair, sewing machine, house, bridge, or locomotive—is an artist." The Plattsville Road Underpass, shown during 1947, mimics the streamline Moderne style Teague introduced to Texaco.

The Madison Avenue Underpass, built during 1939, is an outstanding example of Art Moderne architecture. Faced with scalloped panels and decorative pylons, the Madison Avenue Underpass exhibits a light, airy feeling with vertical lines echoing George Dunkelberger's philosophy that the design should typify the character of the landscape—in rolling country, through the addition of a few verticals. In this photograph, taken by a photographer for the CHD, a natural presence is sensed with the structure blending beautifully into its environment of pine trees and tall grasses.

The abutment faces of the 1936 Main Street Route III Underpass project a clapboarding effect in an attempt to emphasize a horizontal appearance, consistent with George Dunkelberger's belief that a bridge design should blend as much as possible with its location. Prior to choosing a design, Dunkelberger would view the proposed site, taking into account existing contours and surrounding development (including historic features). Often, he would sketch a number of proposals and return to the design office in Middletown to talk them over with other team members.

The 1942 Frenchtown Road Underpass, the last bridge constructed on the Parkway, was built following the outbreak of WW II. Many think the Frenchtown Road Underpass is faced with stone, but its facing consists of precast concrete blocks chemically treated to produce varying shades of buff, tan, or brown. Its center pier with a cutwater design implies a "water bridge" with traffic passing through its portals as a fast-moving stream. Dunkelberger was not particularly fond of its appearance, but declared that "beauty is in the eye of the beholder."

This 1947 CHD photograph shows exit 48 in Trumbull looking westerly. From the date of its initial opening on June 29, 1938, to October 30, 1940, the Merritt enabled approximately 300 million vehicle miles of travel. About 42 percent of this travel was made by out-of-state vehicles. By 1947, so many vehicles had traveled the Parkway that the white concrete pavement had turned black from tire wear, oil drippings, and exhaust fumes. The contrast is very noticeable in the photograph and was the subject of a 1947 research project, which studied vehicle tracking at the Parkway interchanges using aerial photographs.

The 1940 Huntington Turnpike Overpass, demolished during 1979, contained a grille casting in each abutment pylon. Designed to resemble a trellis, the grille with its grapevine was set in front of a recessed niche, the back wall of which was treated chemically to produce a red foil effect. When the Huntington Turnpike Overpass was demolished, the grilles were salvaged, restored, and placed as decorative items on the replacement Huntington Turnpike Underpass, making the grilles visible to Merritt travelers.

The 1935 railroad bridge carries the Housatonic branch over the subgrade of the future Merritt Parkway. It was designed by the CHD and the railroad, with each organization designing elements of the bridge to fit its design standards. The railroad was originally located on a 17-foot man-made site at the Parkway location. During construction of the roadway, the fill was breached and a temporary wood trestle was constructed to carry the railroad through the site. Rocky Hill Road crosses the graded roadway on the near side of the bridge.

A Ford "woodie" heads east on the Parkway during 1948. This view from the Housatonic Railroad Bridge shows Rocky Hill Road crossing the Parkway at grade with stop signs; this condition existed until the road was re-routed during the late 1940s. Rocky Hill Road was relocated and the railroad bridge became a limited-use highway bridge. The open area to the left is an unused portion of the original right-of-way. Running beneath the grass on the right is a long concrete box culvert, built to replace an 1840 stone-arch culvert constructed by the railroad.

Looking eastbound toward Stratford in 1947, the Merritt Parkway curves to the right after passing over the White Plains Road Overpass. This curve, number 43, was the first curve of the original Merritt Highway designed to direct the roadway toward a junction with U.S. Route 1 in Stratford. Subsequent contracts redirected the alignment beyond curve number 43 to a new river crossing 3 miles north of Washington Bridge. The 1947 Merritt Parkway Speed Study recommended the removal of shrubbery at this location following five accidents and two fatalities.

Trumbull has the distinction of harboring the youngest original Parkway underpass (at Frenchtown Road) and the oldest Parkway overpass (at White Plains Road, shown above). Constructed of reinforced concrete and encased steel-girder design during 1934 at a cost of $47,532 and financed by NRA grants and CHD funds, the White Plains Road Overpass is not a typical Parkway structure. It was designed prior to the Parkway concept being adopted in 1934 and reflects the newer state highway bridges seen throughout Connecticut during the early thirties.

104

The 1935 White Plains Road Overpass is shown looking westerly. In the distance a line of trees crosses the cleared Merritt Highway right-of-way, hiding the Housatonic Railroad and the Poquonnock River. During this period, the Connecticut Legislature passed a bill designating the Merritt Highway as a parkway with the provision that Fairfield County would back a $15 million bond issue to complete the entire road from Greenwich to Stratford. In addition, the same legislation amplified the road's grade-separation program. Originally, only the most important intersections were to be bridged.

A 1952 panorama shows the White Plains Road Overpass, the Poquonnock River Bridge, and the former Housatonic branch of the New Haven Railroad. Taken from the same angle as the one above, this photograph illustrates the transformation of a jumble of broken rock and fill to an ordered sequence of pavement and traffic. The grade was critical here and required a minimum elevation for White Plains Road and its ramps from the Parkway without excessive filling. In addition, the road profile required a specified distance over the Poquonnock River and almost immediately sufficient clearance under the railroad bridge.

A variety of 1950s vintage automobiles passes through the twin barrels of the Route 8 Underpass during 1958. Constructed during 1939, this imposing structure was a Parkway landmark for 40 years. Measuring in excess of 150 feet on each face, this underpass had the appearance of a tunnel portal. It was built without a narrowed center park strip, one of three underpasses designed to counter the criticisms of Robert Hurley. Unfortunately, the Route 8 Underpass was demolished during 1979 as part of an improvement project.

This 1938 Trumbull scene captures many construction activities underway. In the distance, workers drilling blast holes create dust as a power shovel loads blasted rock and earth into dump trucks for the filling operations in the foreground. A bulldozer spreads dumped loads and compacts the newly placed fill. Prior to grading operations, a 24-inch concrete-pipe cross-culvert and manhole were completed to convey water from right to left and from future drains on the paved Parkway. At locations where ground water was close to the pavement grade and in rock, side drains were excavated.

Eight

STRATFORD

THIS IS
STRATFORD
ON THE
MERRITT PARKWAY

George Dunkelberger was ever mindful of his audience. During the design process for the Merritt Bridges he stated, "Successful design being a matter of opinion, the criticism of the average person is of great value in as much as the majority of people who see the structure are not college professors, architects, or engineers." The James Farm Road Underpass is a

celebration bridge honoring the Connecticut Highway Department's 45th birthday. The structure of classic design and symbolizing the progressive Connecticut State Highway Department, was completed during 1940. On each pylon is a cameo with the letters CHD. From 1934 to 1940, the Department's bridge engineers designed 358 bridges throughout the state.

Traffic congestion on U.S. Route 1 is shown in West Haven during 1925. This was a common scene that inspired Route 1's nickname, "The Roaring Road." In the confusion of traffic, intersecting roads, speed traps, wayside businesses, scores of traffic signals, unclear signing, stopped delivery trucks, short tempers, and overheated radiators, reaching West Haven was a challenge that ended with frazzled nerves and complete exhaustion. But Route 1 was the only direct route through Connecticut's densely populated urban corridor until 1940 when the Parkway bypassed 11 town centers.

Although construction for the Merritt Parkway began in Greenwich, construction for the Merritt Highway began in Stratford. This view shows the first half-mile of Merritt Highway completed in 1932, constructed 40 feet wide at a minimal cost. To the east of New Haven, Route 80—built as an inland route to alleviate congestion on U.S. Route 1—was being constructed to the same standard. Ironically, Route 80 continues its unspoiled passage through undeveloped countryside while the Merritt Parkway has been compressed by urban development.

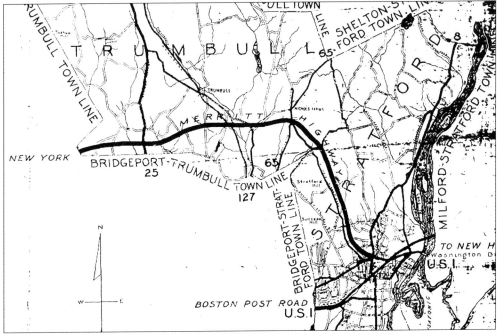

Plans to construct the Merritt Highway through Stratford included a routing parallel to Nichols Farms Road (presently Route 108) and joining U.S. Route 1 at East Main Street. The Merritt Highway traffic merging with the U.S. Route 1 traffic would theoretically cross the Washington Bridge and continue to New Haven. As construction progressed on the Merritt Highway, the Connecticut Legislature passed a bill changing the eastern alignment of the road to a new river crossing referred to as the Housatonic River Viaduct.

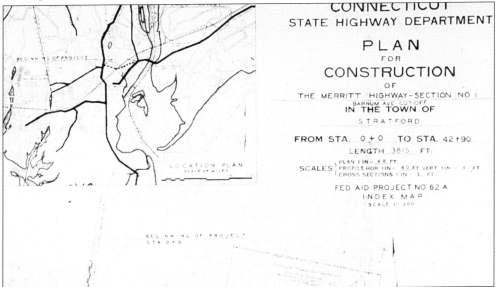

Following the Connecticut Legislature's decision to realign the eastern end of the Merritt Highway 3 miles farther north and to eliminate a bottleneck at the Washington Bridge, the CHD petitioned the U.S. Government to include the newly constructed length of Merritt Highway as a relocated section of U.S. 1. It then became the Barnum Avenue Cut-off.

This 1946 scene shows the end of the Merritt Parkway in the distance as it approaches the Housatonic River Viaduct. The principles of parkway design are evident—the wide, park-like right-of-way, control of access, elimination of grade crossings with other highways, the fitting of alignment and grade to the natural contours of the ground without excessive cuts and fills, the shaping and rounding of slopes to merge them into the adjacent natural land forms, restoration of natural vegetation, and a high standard of architectural excellence for bridges and roadside furniture.

On September 2, 1940, Gov. Raymond Baldwin delivered the keynote speech at the center of the viaduct extolling the Parkway's completion to over one thousand people. Prior to the ceremony, former Gov. Wilbur Cross led a delegation from the Milford end and Louise Merritt (Shuyler Merritt's daughter) led a delegation from the Stratford end. The ladies' high-heeled shoes posed a safety hazard on the open steel deck, and workmen placed plywood sheets for them to walk on. The undeveloped land above and to the left of the viaduct became the future home of Sikorsky Aircraft.

On September 2, 1940, the fourth and last section of the Merritt Parkway was opened for traffic, completing 37.46 miles of divided concrete pavement. The ceremony honoring completion of the Parkway was ironic. The place chosen was the center of the Housatonic River Viaduct—a state-of-the-art design completely lacking aesthetic embellishment compared to the Parkway being celebrated. The viaduct, built as an independent project, was part of the Parkway route and served as a link to the future Wilbur Cross Parkway.

The open-grid steel deck was only one aspect of the viaduct's unique design and construction. On June 8, 1937, the Connecticut Legislature passed Special Act 394, which radically changed the eastern end of the Merritt Parkway and provided for a new river crossing called the Stratford Milford Viaduct. No state funds were appropriated to construct the viaduct, so the CHD applied to the Federal Public Works Administration for assistance. On November 10, 1938, the CHD received a grant of $1 million to design and build the viaduct.

As the winds of war were being felt around the world and the United States was gearing up for conflict, the Housatonic River Viaduct was promoted as a key link in Connecticut's highway system. Indeed during 1943 it was designated a strategic bridge and was accorded a 24-hour armed sentry. Its design was rushed and a condition of its funding stated that a construction contract was to be in force by December 31, 1938. Design plans were approved on November 23, 1938, following a frenzied final design by CHD engineers and the American Bridge Company. A simple but functional design was chosen with minimal dead load, using state-of-the-art, prefabricated open-grid steel decking.

114

Looking west toward Stratford during August 1940, the Housatonic River flows toward Long Island Sound—a picture of tranquillity. Although the lightweight construction was designed with minimal use of concrete that required time-consuming forming and curing, 8 million pounds of steel were used for the superstructure. The main steel girders were fabricated in Pennsylvania, placed on barges, and floated up Long Island Sound to the site. The lightweight open-grid deck quickly became a bane to drivers, causing vehicles to yaw at high speeds. Icing conditions have remained a worry to drivers and a maintenance headache for ice- and snow-control operations.

George Dunkelberger sketched this drawing of a CHD surveyor and his transit for the cover illustration of the 1944 highway Commissioner's "Biennial Report." Behind him and to the left is the planned expansion of the Berlin Turnpike and the Route 72 Overpass in Berlin. To the right is the proposed but never constructed Wilbur Cross Parkway Extension, expected to carry Merritt Parkway traffic to Union as a non-commercial Route 15.

The Merritt Parkway

As tourist traffic increased following WW II, the Gulf Oil Corporation issued a six-page leaflet containing a map of the Parkway and "rules of the road" for its use.

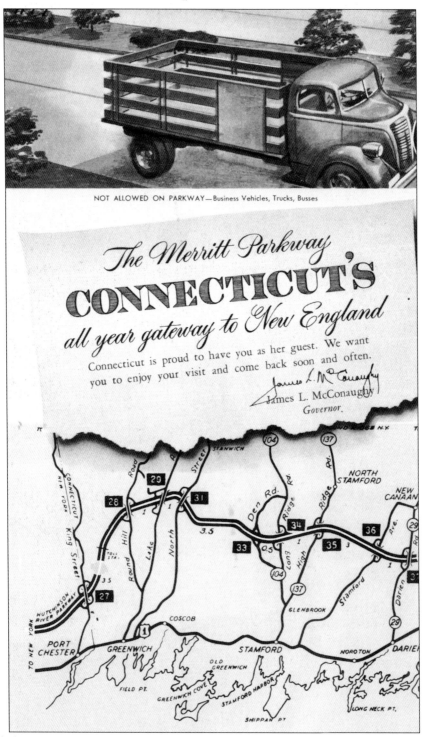

NOT ALLOWED ON PARKWAY—Business Vehicles, Trucks, Busses

The Merritt Parkway

CONNECTICUT'S

all year gateway to New England

Connecticut is proud to have you as her guest. We want you to enjoy your visit and come back soon and often.

James L. McConaughy
Governor.

Issued during 1947, the leaflet listed the newly assigned Parkway exit numbers. Exit 30, Butternut Hollow Road was closed just prior to the map publication date. Exit 32 was never constructed.

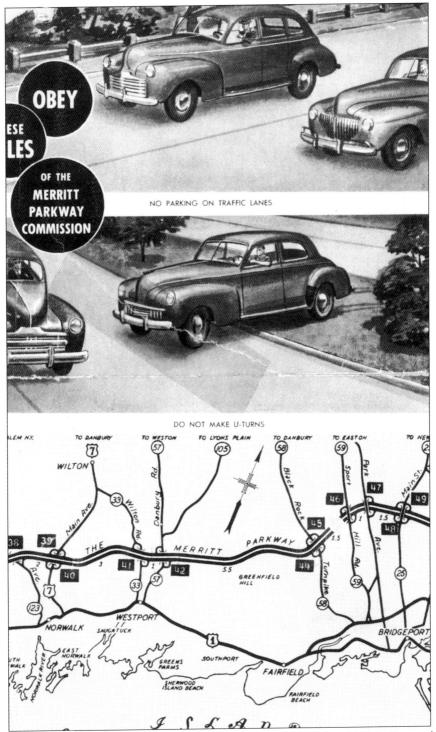

OBEY

ESE

LES

OF THE

MERRITT
PARKWAY
COMMISSION

NO PARKING ON TRAFFIC LANES

DO NOT MAKE U-TURNS

The stretch of Parkway between exit 42 and 44 is called "No Man's Land." Exit 43 was planned but never built after protests from local property owners. Its absence created the longest section of the Parkway without an exit.

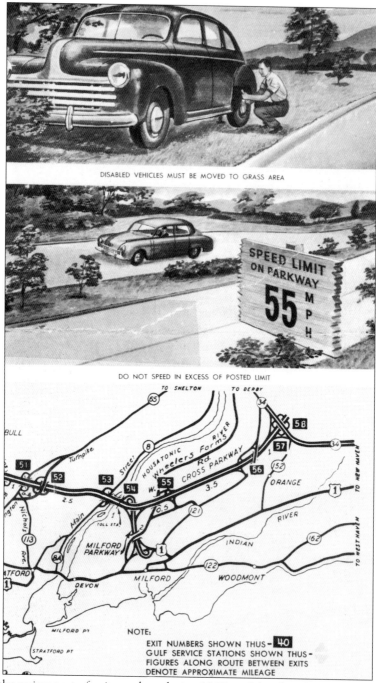

DISABLED VEHICLES MUST BE MOVED TO GRASS AREA

DO NOT SPEED IN EXCESS OF POSTED LIMIT

NOTE:
EXIT NUMBERS SHOWN THUS - 40
GULF SERVICE STATIONS SHOWN THUS -
FIGURES ALONG ROUTE BETWEEN EXITS
DENOTE APPROXIMATE MILEAGE

Following the assignment of exit numbers during 1947, and faced with a new route containing eight different names from Greenwich to Union, the CHD designated this road as Route 15 on May 1, 1948.

Until 1959, traffic on the Parkway was regulated by the Merritt Parkway Commission, a body of nine appointed Fairfield County residents and the CHD Commissioner.

Each payment of 10c Toll is used in the construction of the Wilbur Cross Parkway, which is an extension of the Merritt Parkway.

Courteous, well trained Gulf employees will provide touring information at all Merritt Parkway service stations.

Do not discard papers on Parkway. Do not throw lighted cigarettes. Be considerate.

HELP US KEEP THE PARKWAY CLEAN

If your vehicle becomes inoperative, park on roadside and wait for State Police to secure assistance. Do not hitch-hike.

EXIT 39
NORWALK

For your convenience, all exits have been assigned numbers as shown on the map.

Keep to the Right, except when passing.

These regulations are a condensed text of the complete rules, a copy of which may be obtained from the Merritt Parkway Commission Secretary, Webster U. Walker, 239 Collingwood Road, Bridgeport 4, Conn.

Welcome! By obeying these rules, you will help make Connecticut a good state in which to travel and a better state in which to live.

JAMES MELTON, *Chairman*
The Merritt Parkway Commission

The famous tenor, James Melton of Weston, Connecticut, served as a chairman of the Merritt Parkway Commission until July 1, 1949. He was an avid antique car enthusiast and owned a private museum featuring antique cars and fire trucks.

In 1925, the CHD established a landscape division responsible for tree care, roadside picnic areas, and erosion prevention. The National Industrial Recovery Act Grants of 1933 mandated landscaping on main highways as a demonstration of what could be accomplished to beautify roads. This approach to highway beautification was adopted by the Parkway designers and implemented by the department's landscape division.

This photograph taken on Memorial Day weekend in 1952 from the Milford toll canopy shows Fords, Chryslers, Studebakers, Oldsmobiles, and other vintage cars headed east and north after passing over the Housatonic River Viaduct from Stratford. Traffic in the left-hand lane is heading for U.S. Route 1 and points east, while the remaining traffic is headed north using the Wilbur Cross Parkway. The average tourist driving the Merritt and Wilbur Cross Parkways during the same trip made little distinction between the two. It was a pleasure driving a through route into central New England without the hassles of U.S. Route 1 and U.S Route 5.

As U.S. Route 1 became the historical equivalent of Interstate 95 during the mid-1920s, accidents such as the one shown above became more numerous and deadly in nature. This *c.* 1920 image typifies the collisions that occurred between parallel routes of highway traffic and streetcar interurban traffic. When the Boston Post Road was included as U.S. Route 1 from Florida to Maine during 1926, its importance as a through route connecting the major cities on the eastern seaboard brought a regional traffic impact to Connecticut. Constructing the Merritt Parkway alleviated traffic conditions temporarily, but the road's convenience led to rapid development of Fairfield County.

Nine

THE WILBUR CROSS PARKWAY

The Milford tolls—shown above during 1977—marked the beginning of the Wilbur Cross Parkway until their removal in 1988. Construction of the Wilbur Cross was authorized during 1937 with its beginning at U.S. Route 1. As plans for the Wilbur Cross emerged, the section between Route 1 and the present Wilbur Cross became the Milford Parkway (aka Milford Connector). Many travelers consider the Merritt and its cousin, the Wilbur Cross, as one road. Tolls collected on the Merritt funded the construction of the Wilbur Cross.

This 1949 aerial view shows the southern end of the West Rock Tunnel, the only non-water highway tunnel in New England when it was completed that year. During 1958, this stretch of Parkway was featured in *The Tunnel of Love*, a movie starring Gene Kelly and Doris Day. The decision to tunnel through West Rock rather than build the Wilbur Cross around it was based on economics and prestige. The CHD would be the first in New England to operate a state highway tunnel.

Two drilling jumbos owned by the Gull Contracting Co. are drilling horizontal blast holes on the south heading of the West Rock Tunnel during 1948. This followed the creation of an open cut to expose a vertical face from which the actual tunnel would begin. The tunnel was constructed at a cost of $2 million by Gull Contracting and De Felice Construction Co. Gull Contracting was also building the Brooklyn Battery Tunnel from lower Manhattan to Brooklyn under the East River in New York City.

In a ceremonial gesture on November 8, 1948, Governor Shannon pulled the switch setting off the final dynamite blast to "hole through" the twin-bore tunnel in Woodbridge and New Haven. On November 1, 1949, in the presence of Governor Dewey of New York and Governor Dever of Massachusetts, Gov. Chester Bowles of Connecticut cut a ribbon at one end of the twin tunnels to open the final 8-mile section of the Wilbur Cross Parkway from Derby Avenue in Orange to Dixwell Avenue in Hamden.

Construction workers and bystanders view the final blast that holed through one of the twin bores. The steel lining from the opposite end of the tunnel is just visible in the photograph. During rock removal operations following the holing through, a portion of the tunnel roof collapsed, killing one worker and injuring others. A bronze plaque honoring the worker's efforts is mounted on the south portal facing between the twin bores. The West Rock Tunnel is located approximately 200 feet below the summit of West Rock Ridge.

The Bishop Street Underpass carries Bishop Street (Route 22) over the Wilbur Cross Parkway in North Haven. Designed by the CHD's bridge design unit and George Dunkelberger, this structure was completed during 1947 as a concrete rigid frame. In the distance, another underpass carries Upper State Street over the Wilbur Cross. Most of the underpasses on the Wilbur Cross reflect post-WW II functionalism and lack the creative imagination of the Merritt underpasses. But a new era had dawned; the motorist was traveling faster and was focused on his destination.